Selected Duets

for CORNET or TRUMPET

by H. VOXMAN

Published In Two Volumes:

VOLUME I (Easy - Medium) ● VOLUME II (Advanced)

CONTENTS OF VOL. II:

®RUBANK, INC.

HAL•LEONARD™ CORPORATION

7777 W. BLUEMOUND RD. P.O. BOX 13819 MILWAUKEE, WI 53213

Six Duets

Selected from the Works of Bimboni

BIMBONI

p
3
3
poco rit.
p a tempo
pp
p

RONDO

BIMBONI

2

f
p
p
cresc.
f
p
1
p
cresc.
f
pp

f
p
p
dim.
rit.
Tempo I
p scherzoso
1
p
1

p cresc.
f
Lento
ad lib.
colla parte
Tempo I
p
1
p
1
f

BIMBONI

Allegro risoluto

3

cresc.

p
p
p

risoluto
risoluto
p scherzando

RONDO

Allegro grazioso

BIMBONI

f
p
p
cresc.
p
cresc.
p
cresc.
p
cresc.
Lento
p
p
Tempo I
p
p

Meno

legato
risoluto
Lento
stentate

Tempo I

BIMBONI

Allegretto
Adagio
Tempo I (Allegretto)
dim.
Adagio
dim.
Tempo I (Allegretto)
mf

ff
p
p
f
f
pp

rall.
Tempo I
p
p
Adagio
p
dim.

Meno
pp
f
Tempo I
p
f

Tema

Andante cantabile

BIMBONI

6

Variazione 1a

Poco più

Variazione 2a
Tempo della 1a Variazione
p

Variazione 3a

Tempo della 1a Variazione

Variazione 4a

Adagio

Allegro giusto
p

p
cresc.
cresc. sempre
f

Five Duets

Selected from the Works of Boismortier, Haag, Stamitz, and Telemann

ROMANCE

STAMITZ

GIGUE

HAAG

Allegro

2

f
mp
f
p
cresc.
f

ALLEGRO

(from Canonic Sonata No. 1)

Second player begins when first reaches 𝄋 and ends at the first 𝄐, which should not be observed by the first player.

TELEMANN

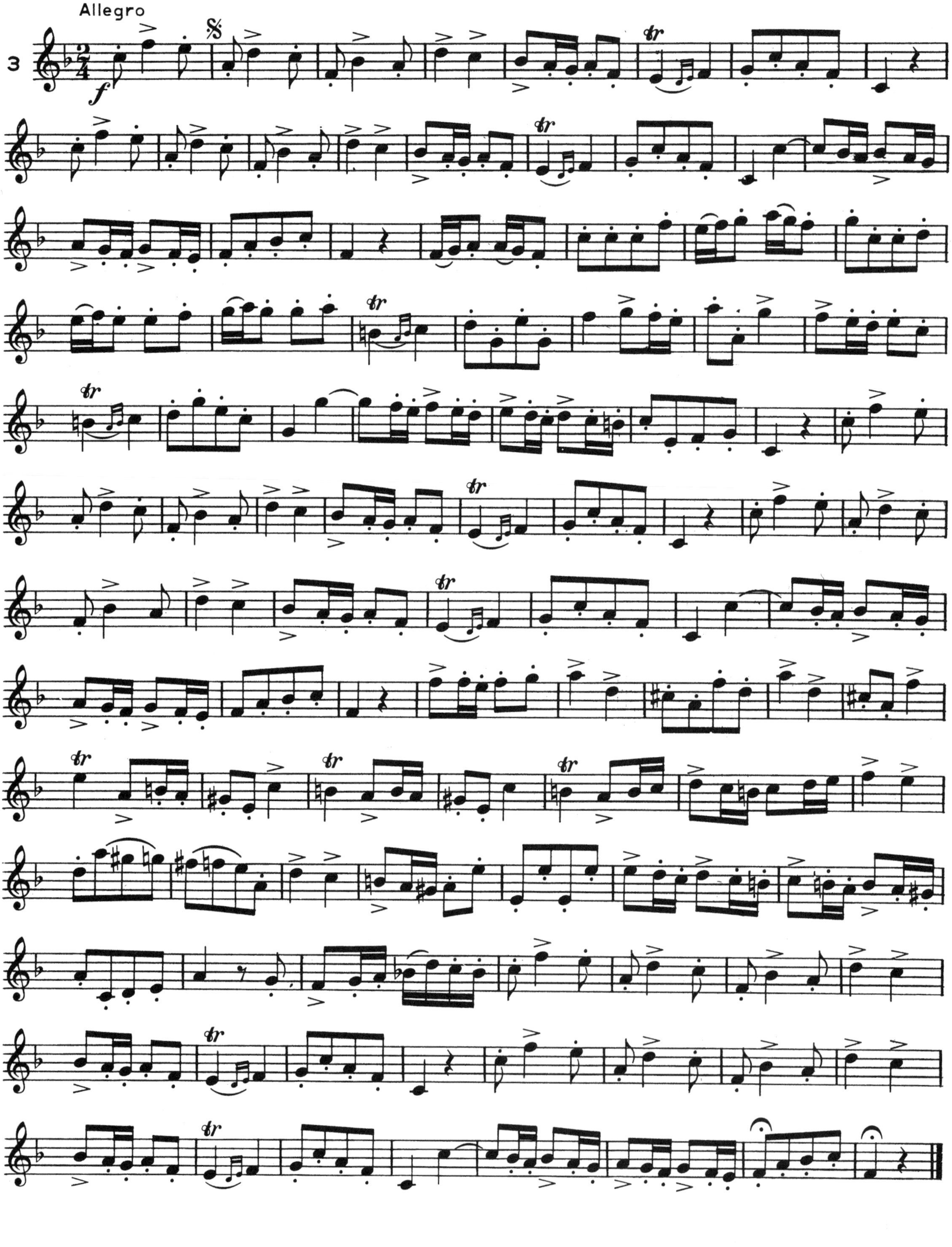

VIVACE

(from Sonata No.4)

TELEMANN

poco rit.

Allegro
5
f
p
tr
poco rit.

Four Duets

Selected from the Works of Gatti

GATTI

1

GATTI

pp rall.
poco a poco
ff
pp leggiero
ff
pp
ff
f
pp
rall. poco a
poco
ff

pp leggiero
p scherzando
f
p
f
p
f
p
ff
cresc.
ff

GATTI

Largo

3

GATTI

Allegro moderato

4

leggiero e scherz.
ff
pp
cresc.
f
p calando e
smorz.
f
p
smorz.
pp

sf
sf
p e cresc.
ff
tutta forza
smorz.
pp espressivo e con grazia
pp
ff
p
ff

p
pp
animando
cresc.
rinf.
ff
pp

pp
cresc.
cresc.
ff
p cresc.
ff
ff
p
smorz.
ppp

Six Duos

Selected from the Works of Clodomir

CLODOMIR

Allegro moderato (♩=120)

1

p
mf
mf
Animato
ff
ff

CLODOMIR

Allegretto (♩ = 104)

2

CLODOMIR

Moderato (♩= 100)

rit.
Tempo I
mf
f

Allegro con moto (♩ = 160) CLODOMIR

f
p
mf
D.C.

Allegretto (♩. = 108)

CLODOMIR

ff
ff
mf
cresc.
ff
pp
pp
ff
ff
p
p
mf D.S. al Fine

CLODOMIR

p
p
Fine
ff
ff
mf
mf
D.S. al Fine

Six Duets

Selected from the Works of Paudert

PAUDERT

p
p dolce
pp
mf
mf
cresc.
cresc.
f
f

p
p
p dolce
f
f
pp
pp
cresc.
f
ff

PAUDERT

Tempo di Polacca

p
p
pp
p
cresc.
cresc.
f
mf

Moderato

PAUDERT

3

cresc.

PAUDERT

cresc.
f
p

f
rit.
p
pp a tempo
ff

PAUDERT

5

mf
f
f
p
p dolce

Allegro moderato

PAUDERT

6

f
pp
p
mf
cresc.
tr